Henry Major Stephenson

Christ

The Life of Men

Henry Major Stephenson

Christ
The Life of Men

ISBN/EAN: 9783744652018

Printed in Europe, USA, Canada, Australia, Japan

Cover: Foto ©Lupo / pixelio.de

More available books at **www.hansebooks.com**

CHRIST THE LIFE OF MEN

THE HULSEAN LECTUR]

BY

The Rev. H. M. STEPHENSON, M.A.

VICAR OF BOURN, CAMBS.

LATE HEAD MASTER OF ST PETER'S SCHOOL, YORK,

FORMERLY FELLOW OF CHRIST'S COLLEGE, CAMBRIDGE.

CAMBRIDGE

AT THE UNIVERSITY PRESS

1890

TO

\

THE FRIENDS IN YORK

TO WHOSE GENEROUS SYMPATHY THE PUBLICATION

OF THESE LECTURES IS DUE

THEY ARE

GRATEFULLY AND AFFECTIONATELY DEDICATED

BY THE AUTHOR.

PREFACE.

I FEEL that I ought to apologise for the title of these Lectures, which are really only fragments of experience in the direction indicated by the title. But a book must have a name, and a long-winded one is inconvenient, an obtrusively modest one, revolting.

H. M. S.

BOURN VICARAGE, CAMBS.
January, 1890.

CONTENTS.

I.

CHRIST THE DIVINE CONSCIOUSNESS IN MEN.

PHILIPPIANS I. 21.

To me to live is Christ.

I CANNOT help thinking that it would sound very strange if not quite unintelligible to us nowadays to hear a man say that to him to live was another man. Modified in some way or other the phrase might sound intelligible, possibly even natural. "To me to live is to study, imitate, expound, venerate another man"—that would be intelligible. But even with this modification, the phrase could probably only have a partial or temporary application or meaning. The word "to live" must itself probably have a limited sense. It could hardly mean the whole life in its whole length and breadth. No man would say of another man that that man occupied his whole existence, and would always do so, even if he only meant by that expression that the man in question in some way filled his thoughts. But

S. L.   1 to say of a man barely and without qualification, 'he is life to me,' 'to live to me is he,' would I think seem so strange as to be almost inexplicable. 'To me to live is Moses, Socrates, Luther,' seems a phrase which could hardly be used at all by any one with respect for language, in order to convey an intelligible sense. At any rate the utmost that could be conveyed by it (assuming it to be intelligible at all) would be something of this kind: 'without the presence of one of these men in my mind as an object of thought, or as exciting emotions of some kind within me, my life would be something different from what it is.' It would be, I think, at best a loose way of saying 'at the present time such and such a man occupies a large part of my thoughts.' Now assuming that the expression could be used merely to·mean this much, are we justified in thinking that that is what St Paul meant by it? Or rather are we justified in thinking that that is *all* that he meant by it?

St Paul's words no doubt include all that would be meant when one man said of another that thoughts about him occupied his mind at all times. They no doubt mean that St Paul lived to preach Christ, to make Him known, to study Him in order to make the knowledge of Him more and more perfect, that all St Paul's life was coloured by his knowledge of Christ, all his actions motived by the thought of Christ. But can that be all that he meant? Would he, if that was all he meant, have used that very remarkable expression, 'to me to live is Christ'? When he could have expressed himself more naturally in some other way, such as 'I live only to preach, or serve or magnify Christ,' would he use a loose or hyperbolical expression which was not necessary? Would he use an expression which had probably never been used before, only to mean that which required no new expression to convey it?

In estimating the answer to these questions, we ought I think to consider (1) the circumstances under which he spoke the words, (2) whether he uses words of similar import in other places and (3) lastly the context of the words in this place.

(1) Now at the time when St Paul spoke these words he was, and probably must have had grave apprehensions that he was, on the eve of departure from this life. If we dismiss what appears to be the untenable theory of his subsequent travels in the west of Europe, he must have been at this time awaiting the trial which resulted in his execution. This is not, one would say, a time when a man indulges in highflown or fanciful or exaggerated expressions about himself.

(2) On the second head I will refer only to one remarkable passage in the Epistle to the Colossians (iii. 21). There urging the Colossians to act on the belief that they had died with Christ, and risen with Him and to let their thoughts rise up to the level of

that belief, and seek to live with Christ in heaven, he encourages them to believe that the truth, the reality, the intrinsic grandeur of that life hidden with Christ in GOD, will one day be fully established. And in doing so he uses the following words 'when Christ *who is our life* shall be manifested, then shall you also be manifested with Him in glory.'

(3) Lastly, as regards the context of these words the sense of the whole passage, in which they occur, seems to be in substance as follows: St Paul is certain that what is happening will result in salvation, which perhaps we might render better negatively, in no loss of life (σωτηρία) to him. His old fearless outspokenness will not fail him, he will not be put to shame: but Christ will be magnified in his person, (not, observe, 'he will magnify Christ' but 'Christ will be magnified in him') whether he continue in the world or be sent out of it. 'As far as I am concerned' he continues 'life here or elsewhere to me is Christ: only life out of this world will perhaps be fuller Christ: personally I would rather go to that fuller fruition of Christ: for your sakes it would perhaps be better that I should stay here.' This appears to me to be in substance the meaning of the passage in which the text occurs, though in giving it thus concisely I have perhaps anticipated somewhat, and assumed without stating, what I take to be a fact about St Paul's use of the words life and death. By death St Paul appears to

mean simply the state which is the result of conscious sin, or separation from GOD. Life without GOD is death. Life with GOD is life. Physical life and death are quite subordinate in his mind to this real life and death, mere accidents of them, external conditions or expressions or perhaps even symbols of them. The physical life with the living intercourse, the communion which it necessarily implies, is the symbol of that communion in which the real life consists. The separation and isolation implied in physical death identifies it with the separation which makes the real death. So completely is this the case, so completely in St Paul's mind are physical life and death embraced within the real life and death, that he is not at pains to distinguish them sometimes, where the distinction would have made his meaning clearer, but passes insensibly from the one meaning to the other *quasi desultorius* in the same passage, thinking now more of the physical aspect of death, now of the spiritual, of resurrection now as the continuation of consciousness, now as the recovery from a state of separation from GOD. As an example of this I would point (besides the passage in which the text occurs) to the very remarkable passage in the Epistle to the Romans v. 12–15.

If this be a correct statement of the meaning which St Paul attached to life, and he says that to go on living in the body is to him Christ, he must surely

mean that Christ to him is life in the only full sense he
recognised, that is, communion with GOD, union with
the Father-Spirit, that Christ in other words is the
Word of GOD to him, that Being by whom all the
words of GOD come to men, the Bread of life on which
alone their life can be supported, the Being through
whom men's spirits come into harmony with the Spirit
on which all true existence depends, the Being through
whom the spirit of man is led into all truth. It would
seem then that St Paul believed (1) not only that it is
possible for the human spirit to be consciously united
to GOD, therefore to know GOD, but (2) that such union
is possible through Christ, that (to put it as he puts it)
Christ is to men that union with GOD. This seems
to be a mere truism, a platitude of the flattest, a
commonplace of theology. But yet there is, I fancy,
some tendency nowadays to avoid it, to gently ignore it
in its naked proportions. There is, I fear, a tendency
on the part of Christians to acquiesce in a sort of
orthodox agnosticism (if I may venture to use a word
which has been appropriated by extra-Christian philosophers, assuming of course that such a Protean word
can be said to be appropriated at all). The tendency
of ordinary Christian thought and (if I may use the
term) of the ordinary pulpit seems rather to deal with
Christianity than with Christ, to dwell on the Gospel
as the revelation of a higher morality rather than as
the revelation of the source of all morality, as the

revelation of a scheme of redemption for a lost world, rather than as the revelation of the redeeming GOD, as a certain amount of knowledge about Himself revealed through Christ and by Him entrusted to a church for the guidance of men, a regulative revelation, an improved Law in fact, rather than the absolute unveiling of Himself in the Word made flesh.

The large occupation, the almost concentration of theological study on what I venture to call the lendings of the Gospel, the critical study of documents, of contemporary literature, of historical and geographical detail connected with it, of general ecclesiastical history, of church politics, seems likely to assist the tendency I speak of. GOD forbid that I should impugn the usefulness of those studies—it would be absurd to do so—or that I should fail to acknowledge that some of the most distinguished leaders in those branches of study are at the same time profound theologians in the true sense, men penetrated with the deepest conviction of the full and absolute nature of the revelation of GOD in Christ. But there may be a temptation to give too exclusive attention to these studies, and this may draw away from the inner fact of the Gospel itself, from the actual voice of the Word of GOD speaking in it. That may be especially a temptation in days when supernatural religion is much more easily tolerated by the world if it keep clear of reason, when a revelation which merely prescribes a rule of conduct, the grounds of which are veiled in mystery, is treated with much more respect by logicians and philosophers than one which claims to declare the mind of GOD to finite creatures. But if this tendency should prevail, it would mean that we should have to be content with a religion which is divorced from reason, with a revelation which only declares the necessity for certain conduct of thought and action under pains and penalties for disobedience, and has nothing to say to the faculty in man which searches for truth, a revelation which forbids search into the nature of that which is revealed, a religion which lets men speak to GOD only through one small chink opened they know not why, a revelation which reveals not the express image of the Father, but a glimpse of the purposes of GOD, mysterious and inexplicable, outside the human reason, a religion which declares the search for theologic truth to be something different in kind from the search for scientific truth, a revelation not explaining, but excluding all other revelations. This would be but a melancholy remnant of Christianity such as St Paul knew it. It would be almost better to give up Christianity altogether than be content with such a tantalising phantom of revelation as such agnosticism would vouchsafe us. For if Christ is to be our life as He was St Paul's, it is surely essential to that view of our relation to Christ, it must form the basis of that relation in our minds, that we should believe that through Him we know GOD. We

must surely be allowed to see in Him the revealer of
the Father; more than that, the image of the Father,
the Word-GOD speaking with man, not simply the
principal actor in a scheme of redemption, the doler
out of such scant portion of knowledge of the purposes
of GOD as may be sufficient to regulate men's conduct,
a seeing leader of the blind, guiding them in all ignorance. We shall ask to be allowed to see in Him the
discloser of the mind of the Father towards the sons of
His creating, the giver of a Spirit which leads into all
truth, truth of human nature and outside nature, as
well as truth of human conduct. It is difficult to see
how we should be satisfied with less. For those who
look to find in the Gospel the revelation of a Father in
a Son must look to find in the nature of the Father
there revealed the key to those truths which 'in manhood darkly join,' to find reason, for example, why righteousness does tend to happiness for men, and why men
tend on the whole to righteousness; why self-sacrifice is
the highest happiness of human nature; why suffering is
good and not evil, whether it be suffering for our own or
others' sins, or whether it be suffering in pursuit of truth.

Let me confine myself to the first of those questions
which I have exemplified as questions which the
Christian looks to the Gospel for help to answer, Why
does righteousness tend to the happiness of men and
why do men tend on the whole to righteousness rather
than unrighteousness?

There is, as it seems to me, one philosophic theory that seems to touch the root of this truth (if we may assume it to be a truth), one that seems to go below the surface, to give our belief some hold in solid ground, not leave it planted rootless and insecure, one which seems to give us security that this truth may not be at any time reversed, that it may not be declared a falsehood and the tendency of men's thoughts and actions set the other way. The theory that does this for us, unless I am mistaken, is that which claims relation between man's consciousness and an eternal consciousness, between man's spirit and the Spirit which is GOD. A theory this, which has shown great vitality, which has survived the most deadly shocks, and revived again and again from exhaustive philosophic extinction, a theory which but lately found one of its ablest exponents in a member of the sister University whose premature loss so many earnest hearts who knew his guidance have deplored[1]. The other and more popular philosophies to one who seeks firm footing for thought and conduct, who asks for a foundation on which to plant his belief, seem all to fall short just where he wants most to go on. When it comes to the question, why should man be capable of any knowledge at all, why should he be capable of righteous conduct, what has he in virtue of which he can use the terms 'right' and 'wrong,' what has he to assure him that they are

[1] T. H. Green, 'Prolegomena to Ethics.'

what he thinks they are, what has he to assure him
that their significance may not be changed, that evil
may not at any time be enthroned in the place of good,
and all the suffering for what we now call righteousness
sake be proved after all to be so much wasted pain,
when it comes to this question, they seem to have
nothing to say. In fact all that they can do is to tell
us that we can know nothing for certain about such
matters, and to rebuke the presumption of even seeming
to try to get to the bottom of things. The spiritualist
theory does offer an answer to such questions. It
seems to prove in what direction the true answer to
those questions lies.

Showing that the consciousness in man alone makes
a world of experience possible to a man, because it
alone can hold together those relations of which all
experience must consist, it infers that that consciousness
must be something quite different in nature from the
phenomena, out of which it forms its experience, that it
cannot come into being as an affection of those organs
which convey the phenomena out of which the consciousness forms nature for itself, that it must have an
independent existence, an eternal existence independent
of time and space, as that to which related phenomena
and successive events are present together. The very
existence of nature for us, inasmuch as it exists for us
only through the consciousness, implies that that
consciousness is not natural nor the product of nature.

It cannot be the result of the processes which itself originates. However much it may be materially conditioned, however much it may need the body which is organic to its functions, it cannot be material, or derived from its material conditions. To derive it out of that which has no existence without it, is to derive it out of nothing. Further, if men are capable of any knowledge at all, it must be by learning to perceive a single and unalterable order of relations. As error consists in mistaking one set of relations for another, so knowledge is the apprehension of the true relations between things, which true relations form an unalterable system of relations, the same always under the same conditions, an eternal order of things. But how can such an unalterable order of relations exist? It can only exist in virtue of a principle which, like the consciousness in man, can hold plurality in unity, hold the many together in one, make a whole out of many parts, and so constitute relations. And this consciousness, if it is the cause of a single and unalterable order of relations, must be itself one and unalterable, the same yesterday to-day and for ever, an eternal Spirit, other than the nature which exists in virtue of its creating power. And if knowledge of what is real is to become acquainted with this eternal and unalterable order, how is it possible, except by strict affinity between his consciousness and that eternal consciousness, by the imparting of that Eternal Spirit to man? One in that essential power to hold together in unity the different elements of relations, man's consciousness must be akin to that eternal consciousness. But inasmuch as it is conditioned by material conditions, inasmuch as it must learn to know that unalterable order through a distorting haze of sensuous perceptions, the communication cannot be complete as we are constituted here. But communication there must be or we should be incapable of the simplest act of human learning. This theory seems to give some hope to the human being that he may really know in a proper sense of the word, offers him reason why he should so hope, offers him reason why he may hope that the idea of good to which men seem to be struggling, will, when completely realised, prove absolute good; and that being human beings, sharers of the Eternal Consciousness, they are bound to struggle on in the same direction.

But surely this theory needs completing, wants humanising (if I may use the term slightly out of its ordinary sense). If that Eternal Consciousness is imparted to man, surely there must be some Being in whom it is so imparted, some Being akin to man in whom men, if they know Him, recognise that consciousness working under conditions of human organisation, and working perfectly. Surely if the Eternal Consciousness, of which man partakes, is GOD the creator, the Eternal Father, there must be a Son-GOD, and GOD-Man, in whom man partakes of that consciousness, who is that consciousness in every man, who, when mankind have reached their high ideal, the image in which they were created, will be all in all men. And if a man appeared on earth the story of whose life we are told on at least respectable authority, authority as good as most of that on the strength of which we feel calm about the facts of all but quite modern history, if a man appeared on earth who claimed to be such a being, who said of Himself 'I and my Father are one,' who said ' No man knoweth the Father save the Son and he to whom the Son will reveal Him,' who said 'The Father hath delivered all judgment to the Son,' who told His disciples that He was going to His Father who is greater than He, and that if He went away He would send to them the Spirit that should lead them into all truth ; if a man appeared upon earth, who (as men, who cannot have been fools, apparently believed) possessed mastery over the hidden processes of nature, to whom the truths were open secrets which science slowly reveals,—science which owes to Him the inspira- tion of fearless truth-seeking, by which alone it can effectually work (for if there had been fearless truth- seekers before Him, there had been none that could inspire fearlessness)—who on the showing not of His friends, but His enemies, at least anticipated some of the final triumphs of medical psychology, and lit up meteor-like the path along which that science alone can travel to success ; if a man appeared upon earth

who, to one possessed of the profound insight with
which the writer of the Fourth Gospel appears to have
been endowed, seemed to show evident tokens that in
Him dwelt the glory of the only-begotten Son of GOD,
of whom St Paul in spite of the prepossessions and
prejudices of early training believed that He was 'in
the Form of GOD', that there was in Him that which
made Him GOD, though He took on Him the nature of
man, a servant of GOD; if a man appeared upon
earth who by His death has been ever since drawing
men up to Him, whose influence has profoundly modified the thought and conduct of civilised peoples, and
modified them in the direction of the higher self-
sacrificing type of manhood, whose influence shows
itself in those who deny His claims, who cannot accept
His divinity but have received from Him a humanity
which they never could have had without Him;—if
such a man appeared on earth, is He not the Being in
whom was made manifest the Eternal Consciousness, the
Eternal Righteousness, which is Divine and Human
too?

II.

CHRIST THE SOURCE OF LIVING CONDUCT.

PHILIPPIANS I. 21.

To me to live is Christ.

LAST Sunday I suggested that, if Christ is to be the life of men now, as St Paul said He was his life, it is absolutely necessary, in order to realise that relation between Christ and us, that we should be able to recognise Him as the revealer or the revelation of GOD, as the Being in whom the Eternal Spirit, the self-existent Consciousness who makes the Universe possible, is communicated to men, as the giver of the Spirit which leads into all truth. That seems to me to be a necessary preliminary and essential condition of finding life in Christ, that we should regard Him as the Being through whom men become conscious of GOD, become conscious of a divine life, which is outside of them and within them, a life which is, so to say, its own knowledge, which is known in working it out under the material conditions in which men exist, in aspiring to fuller and ever fuller union with Christ.

Assuming this as the basis of all realisation of our life in Christ, I would venture to suggest today another aspect of that life, a practical aspect. I would venture to point out a fact of our everyday lives with which the truth of life in Christ may help us to deal, a difficulty which it may help us to confront, possibly to master. The fact I mean, is the difficulty which most, if not all, of us find in really living our lives, in keeping ourselves morally and spiritually alive, not allowing ourselves to sink into a state of torpor, or at best of somnambulism broken only by intervals of active and conscious moral and spiritual life. To everyday human beings it is a real difficulty to sustain their conduct at the aery level of active, conscious, moral life, to prevent its sinking into the dull earthy atmosphere of passive and monotonous routine. The everyday life of everyday mortals does tend so terribly to routine, to mere reflex moral action. Even the formation of habits so absolutely necessary to virtuous conduct exposes us to this danger more or less.

The constant repetition of the sights and sounds which is involved in the formation of a habit deadens the impressions that these sights and sounds made on us once, and should make on us always, if we are really living our lives. As Bishop Butler in his Chapter on moral discipline says: "From our very faculty of habits, passive impressions by being repeated grow weaker: thoughts by often passing through the mind are felt less sensibly: being accustomed to danger begets intrepidity, i.e. lessens fear: being accustomed to distress, lessens the passion of pity, to instances of others' mortality, lessens the sensible apprehension of our own". And again: "Perception of distress in others is a natural excitement passively to pity and actively to relieve it: but let a man set himself to attend to, inquire out and relieve distressed people and he cannot but grow less and less sensibly affected, with the various miseries of life with which he must become acquainted: when yet at the same time benevolence considered not as a passion, but as a practical principle of action, will strengthen: and whilst he passively compassionates the distressed less, he will acquire a greater aptitude actively to assist and befriend them".

The point that Butler here is speaking to is of course different. He is discoursing on the necessity for active exercise in order to form habits, to qualify ourselves for states of life, for which we were before unqualified, and on the uselessness of mere theorising or contemplation, which tends rather, by the familiarity which it begets, to render us more and more insensible to moral considerations. Still the other inference holds good, that the very formation of habits which make us capable of prompt and steady moral action, whenever occasion calls for it, tends to kill in us that living sympathy with nature, or with men which we have when we begin to form the habit, tends to lessen the sensitive capacity for the impressions which nature and mankind produce in the untrained mind, tends therefore to make our action spontaneous reflex action, the action of moral machines, rather than of living beings throbbing with the excitement of a quick and living sympathy. The very means by which we save our souls the detriment of too much friction, the systematic action which prevents the wear and tear of the spirit felt by the novice who is forming his habits by daily new experiences, these at the same time that they save life destroy it. Because we do not die daily, we do not live fully. Because our souls no longer sink under the awe which nature once struck into us, because we have learned to master the weakness which others' weakness used to stir in us, because we no longer burn when others are offended, because in a word we have cooled and hardened the feelings that used to be warm and soft into the solid material of active habits and systematic practice, we have thereby lost part of our life. The student of nature who has formed his method and habits of research through familiarity with the inexhaustible wonders that nature constantly reveals, tends to lose in the friction of a throng of details the fresh and living sense of wonder, the religious awe which those marvels would once awake in him. Those whose profession, or whose sense of duty engages

them in efforts to ameliorate the condition of their
fellowbeings, by constant familiarity with the scenes
which furnish the materials of their benevolent habits
and their philanthropic system—scenes of all kinds,
from the scenes of large city-life with its morbid
inflammatory activity, to those of village life with its
fenlike stagnation of mind and spirit—are in danger of
losing the vivid sense of pity which such phenomena
should excite, even while they are learning to attack
successfully the evil of them. Even as they learn
their business as practical philanthropists they tend to
regard human life as a matter of business, as material
mainly for philanthropic organisation.

Thus may even our best habits be the means of
weakening the principle of spiritual livingness within
us. And if this is true of our disinterested and benevolent habits, if familiarity tends to turn the exercise
of them into routine work, how much truer is it of
those necessary duties of our everyday life, of that more
or less necessarily self-regarding work, livelihood work,
which makes up such a large portion of the lives of
most of us. There are two reasons of course why such
work constantly tends to become lifeless, to lose all life
and energy, to become mere dead second-hand work,
reflex action only, not the result of conscious impulse
within us, of moral energy, but the dead work of a
machine that works without head or heart. (1) There
is the same reason that is at work in the formation of

our benevolent habits. The constant repetition of the same actions tends to dull the interest of them and even the sense of responsibility in performing them. We get to perform them better and more easily, but as they require less effort to perform, so do we tend to bestow no conscious effort upon them. We all know the difference it makes when we begin new work, enter on new duties, how keenly alive we are to their requirements, how we rouse our energies to perform them. And we know how different it is apt to be when that new work has become old work, how much we are in danger of losing heart in it, performing it lifelessly, losing interest in it, letting it work itself, as a wheel turns round after the force that set it going is removed. (2) And the second reason is that such routine work is in the main self-regarding work only; in so far as it is livelihood work, we have only ourselves to consider in it. We are obliged to do it for the sake of its results: we must do it or else either forego the necessaries of life, or surrender our independence. Now if in the case of those disinterested and benevolent habits, in our self-imposed duties, familiarity and repetition have a tendency to deaden, to rob us of quick and living responsiveness to the sights and sounds of universal nature, ten thousand times more so is it the case with the routine of necessary duties, with the purely biotic life.

The life of disinterested and benevolent duties

though it may lose some of its vitality and living force, can never be killed outright, it can never absolutely die, simply because it *is* disinterested. It has a principle of life in its altruistic aim that will always prevent its stiffening into dead routine. But the livelihood work is continually in danger of becoming wholly self-regarding, egoistic, selfish, wholly dead therefore as far as any conscious moral life, any living solid addition to the life of the worker is concerned. For it is, I take it, a well-known law of human work that if it is not to be mere chaff and draff, mere refuse encumbering not helping, choking not feeding the soul, it must be done for its own sake and the sake of the objects of it, not for the sake of what is gained from it. Work done merely to gain bread or avoid punishment is of no solid value to the worker, contributes nothing to his real life. He who works merely to live, is dead while he lives, is self-condemned 'propter vitam vivendi perdere causas'.

Now such death as this will no doubt be prevented by having some disinterested work (the work being of course important and useful in itself) of our choice, some work we love for its own sake, which we cannot love for external reward to be got from it, whether it be reward of money or reward of praise or reward of power. For experience, I think, shows that having some such preference work, if it be genuine and rightly used, acts as a leaven on the whole life; that it forms

a principle which pervades all the life's work and
assimilates it to that work of love. Those who can
keep their routine work most alive, who do it most
unsordidly and best, are those surely who cherish and
keep by them some work of their own love and choice,
in which their minds can always find rest and freedom.
And the proof that this is genuine and self-rewarding
work is found in its effects on the rest of the life and
on the routine livelihood work. We most of us unfor-
tunately know people who can do any work better than
the work they are paid to do, who must shirk or slur
the work of their vocation because their genius will
carry them fluttering after almost any other work. But
nothing can be more conclusive proof that that other
work is an affectation or a dilettantism or a selfishness
or a sham, than the fact that it has no effect on the
rest of the life's work, or rather has a baneful effect, that
it deadens instead of giving life. No! so surely as a
little leaven leavens the whole lump, so surely will any
genuinely self-forgetful and self-rewarding work of love
react on the whole life's work and make it more or less
like itself. The antidote then to the narcotic influence
of the livelihood routine work would seem to be to
have some work of choice and love, some disinterested
work, done at least for itself and not for external
reward, not for pence or praise, whether it be students'
work of research and speculation into truths which it
concerns men's welfare to know more and more of, not

truths which it pays to learn by heart; or whether it be active work in the midst of men and women, practical work of helping others to rid their lives of falsehoods. Some such work as this hidden in the soul will leaven the life and spread its reality over all the conduct, making all like itself; like leaven it will fill the whole with vital air, like salt it will save the whole from corruption; a guardian work it will be to keep watch over the rest, and save it from the attacks of death.

'Sed quis custodict ipsum custodem?' who or what will guard the guardian work itself against the attacks of the powers of death? what will keep it up to its own high level? what will preserve it wholly alive? what will guard it against weariness and ambition? what will answer the questions that those two will suggest: 'why should I go on working to weariness? where will it end? on what is it based? what is my guarantee that it is not all a mistake? a subjective delusion? How do I know that there is any truth beneath it all? How do I know that it is not a mere fancy that such work may bring its own reward? I know that sometimes I find satisfaction in it. But more often I find disappointment, vexation of spirit, loneliness, as the result of work. Why should I not give up an ideal which only makes me feel my own weakness? Why should I not work for what seems to make others happy? For money, for place, for power, for applause? why should I believe that it is best to live for an idea? why should I not fall back on the material life of comfort, pleasure, excitement? what can answer questions like this? what can guard us against the deadening effect of repetition on our higher lives? what can keep us alive to all those impressions on which the habits of our higher lives are formed? what can keep our hearts soft? prevent their hardening as our habits of action grow settled and solid?

And above all, what is to save us from the load of irresponsibility that weighs upon us, if we attempt to live the higher life, to work the disinterested work that is to keep our lives alive? What can answer, for example, such thoughts as these: "I cannot do this work by myself: other men can help me by advice, by example, by encouragement: they may stimulate me by the knowledge of their needs, by the sense of what they may gain if I exert myself: but this is not enough for me: I can work with them: I can work for them: but I cannot work under them in this my own life's work. They cannot bear that burden for me: 'every man must bear his own burden': and I cannot work under myself: I cannot be my own master: I cannot offer my work to myself: I cannot seek my own perfection to satisfy myself: for then I have nowhere to lay my imperfections: no possibility of rest: nowhere to acquiesce. But a master I must have or give up my life's work: some one who claims my utmost and my best, and yet will take my ragged fragments for what

they are worth : some one who demands my work, yet
is the greatest reward that work can find, one whose
approval I can receive as freely as I receive my own
without loss of independence, self-respect, or disinterested aim, some one who will yoke me, harness me,
control me, guide me, be responsible for me, in whose
mastery I can find repose " ?

I believe there is an answer to all these perplexities
in St Paul's words ' To me to live is Christ '.

If He is the Being through whom the eternal truth
is conveyed to man, if He is the revelation of GOD who
makes all things what they are, then His manhood is
the truth of all manhood. His life upon earth seen by
men and recorded by respectable authorities, is the true
life of all, the pattern life guaranteed by the Incarnate
Truth. And what do we find in that life ? We find
a continuous and unexhausted energy of beneficent
and disinterested action combined with quick and living
sympathy. A life always sustained up to the same
level, undisturbed by ambition, weakness, or mono-
tony : a life intensely real in every part of it : full
and fresh and continuously creative in every action,
marvellously free from all that is second-hand or
adopted in thought or action ; we find the sustained
living energy of one who not only never tired of His
high ideal of communion with GOD, but rested weary
limbs and fed a hungry frame with prayer, we find the
vital enthusiasm of one whose every action was instinct

with life from a living law within, an enthusiasm which
burst into a flame of resentment at all unreality, all
formulated second-hand conduct that came across its
path; we find the living unresting intellect that never
ceased gazing into the real conditions and relations of
things and grasped and knew the secret of creation.
We find a marvellous energy overwhelming in its
greatness—more than human we should say, but that
He in whom it was, was man. And when I speak of
energy, I need not, I think, in this congregation ask
not to be misunderstood or warn my hearers that I do
not mean the spurious thing that in the general world
sometimes goes by the name of energy. There is
such a spurious thing. A restless morbid craving to
be seen working or seeming to work, a fluttering
egotism that can do nothing quietly or in secret,
that desires above all things the reputation of working,
and will work if the reputation is not to be otherwise acquired, a diseased convulsive activity, a sort
of moral chorea. This of course is not true energy.
That is essentially calm and self-contained. It is to the
moral or mental constitution what perfect health is to
the physical, the highest development of the moral and
mental force, ever at work performing its natural
functions but without self-consciousness, as the healthy
body is unconscious of its health. We find, I say, a
marvellous energy of sustained thought, action, and
sympathy in the man Christ Jesus. And this man

is the pattern man, the type of true humanity revealed by GOD in a man.

But He is more than that, if St Paul's words are true and He is the life of men. He is the Divine manhood in men. He is the knowledge of GOD in men. Through Him the eternal consciousness is imparted to men. He is the author of the faith in men by which they see GOD, see Him in the divine life, the Christ life, of which they are certain that it is the true life because it *is* the Christ life, which they live by hiding their life with Christ in GOD. And more, He is the sender of the Spirit from the Father, the Spirit of adoption, the Spirit which makes men feel themselves sons of GOD, brothers of the GOD man, the Spirit by whom the Father and the Son enter into a man, and make their abode with him, the Spirit who makes a man feel his sonship to the Father in partaking of the will-surrender of the Son, and feeling his sonship long to be at one with the Father in the Son, long to feel his sins continually remitted in the effort after peace and union with the Father.

And lastly, He is the King of men. His revelation of the Father was the revelation of a kingdom which is not of this world, the kingdom of the Heavens. He is a King who exercises over His subjects the all powerful control of a will perfectly surrendered to His Father in Heaven ; who exercises a mastery over them, which makes them independent, sets a yoke on them, which eases their shoulders, imposes service on them, which is perfect freedom. For He gives His subjects the means of obedience in offering them the means to a self-surrender such as His, He gives them His flesh and blood to eat and drink, that they may lose their lives in Him, in Him be united with the Father and find ETERNAL life.

I cannot conclude today without reference to the event which was occupying our minds so recently last Sunday, the death of the Provost of King's.

It is a question I suppose whether a life on earth so long as his is a blessing to be craved or not. In many instances, life so far prolonged beyond the ordinary human term, can only be a burden. But if there were a case in which it could safely be pronounced enviable, it would surely be his who was privileged to watch over at College the sons and sons' sons of those whom as boys he had helped to train and form at school, who lived to see reforms in his College initiated by himself bear rich fruit, who, above all, retaining to the end the full use of a highly cultivated intellect found in his later years the weaknesses of extra-normal age strengthened and solaced by the loving ministrations of devoted children, and knew that, however long deferred the end might be which should bring to him the gain of fuller life in Christ, it would, when it came, make a gap in the lives that ministered to his, and steal an occupation of love from those he loved.

III.

CHRIST THE KEY TO THE SUFFERINGS OF LIFE.

PHILIPPIANS I. 21.

To me to live is Christ.

THERE is one fact which meets all of us in the conduct of life, a fact we need some help to live against. It is a fact which sometimes staggers and baffles us in our attempts to live. I mean the existence of suffering in the world, especially of what may humanly speaking be called innocent suffering. That is I suppose an obvious distinction of suffering, into guilty and innocent, suffering, that is, which is apparently the result of transgression and conscious offence, punishment-suffering in a word, and that which cannot be traced to such a source. Both naturally divide themselves again into two classes, bodily and mental. But the latter of the two, innocent suffering, may otherwise be divided into two classes of suffering. There is suffering that comes from within, that comes

from a man himself. There is suffering that comes
from without, comes from others. The suffering that
comes from within arises from the very condition of the
human soul. It is the suffering of a being capable of
longings and aspirations which it is incapable of ful-
filling and satisfying. The suffering that comes from
without comes not always in the same way. It may
come directly from others, as when it comes in the
shape of inherited weakness or inherited propensities;
or when it comes from the conduct or fortunes of
others, which owing to special circumstances of connexion, kinship, proximity of any kind, necessarily
cause pain and trouble to us; when for example
those, who are bound to us by the closest ties that
link human beings together, fall into dishonour or
calamity, or are suddenly and prematurely torn away
from us. Suffering from without may come less
directly, as when the general tendency of the conduct of those among whom we move is to put
obstacles in the way of high moral action, to make
moral progress difficult, to obscure the beauty of the
higher life, to depress our spiritual ambition and 'hang
a weight upon our heart in its assumptions up to
heaven'. Less directly still, suffering from without
comes when our sympathies and experiences widen,
and the sins and misfortunes of others beyond our
own narrower circle become part of our burden, oppress
us with the sense of shared distress, not perhaps with

the keener pangs of kindred shame, kindred privations,
or kindred bereavement, but still with real suffering
and suffering which becomes more real the more our
benevolence widens and deepens.   For this is perhaps
one of the most mysterious facts about mental suffering, without the revelation of Christ a staggering and
hopeless fact, that the capacity for it increases with the
nobleness of the suffering mind.   This is true of all
mental suffering innocent or guilty.   The pain of
remorse is in inverse proportion to the animalism of
the being who feels it.   In the purely stagnant ox-like
nature it can hardly be felt.   The pain of bereavement
is proportioned to the power of loving, the sense of
kindred shame to the keenness of the sense of honour.
But it is more essentially true of what may be called
vicarious suffering, the suffering which comes by sympathy with the sufferings of others, by feeling as our
own the sufferings which from any cause come upon
others.   It is more than ever true of this kind of
suffering.   The nobler, purer, wider and stronger the
philanthropy of a benevolent soul, the greater is its
capacity, the larger (if I may say so) its demand for
suffering.   And as at present at any rate the supply
seems inexhaustible, the larger therefore will be the
amount of suffering such a soul will endure.   So that
assuming no alteration in the law of human progress,
it would almost seem that, if suffering is ever to cease,
it must be by all from the lowest natures upwards

being trained and lifted through who knows what experiences to the highest capacity for the highest suffering. For then suffering would merge in the universal sympathy of noble souls.

This suggests, I think, an exception that may be taken to what I have been saying. It may be urged that, though all these classes of suffering are called by the same name, they really differ in kind. For example the suffering (it may be urged) which may be called vicarious, though related to guilty suffering as product to producer, is yet essentially different from it, as different as ether from the alcohol and acid that generate it. This is probably true; or true so far as this, that there is a suffering which is not strictly speaking punitive nor disciplinary, suffering which belongs to the highest condition of which the human soul is capable, which takes a man away from himself and seems inseparably connected with the highest ideal of human conduct of which the mind is capable. May I by way of illustrating this briefly review some of the views about suffering held by two representative peoples of antiquity, the Greeks and the Hebrews?

In the earlier subjective poetry of the Greeks we find this phenomenon recognised, the existence of unmerited suffering in its various forms. This recognition finds expression either in pure pessimism, or in bewildered complaints about the divine government of the world; or sometimes there is a half heroic, half

sullen acquiescence in what seemed the caprice or the
indifference of the ruling powers ; but combined with
this a dogged determination, when at their best, to
persevere in what seemed to be the better course in
spite at least of ordinary injustice or ordinary selfishness on the part of the controllers of men's destinies.
" Best of all for denizens of earth not to be born at all,
never to see the rays of the piercing sun. Next best
when born to speed us with all haste through the gates
of death ". "O Zeus I wonder at thee: Lord of all thou
art, sovereign potentate in thy own right! Thou
knowest the heart and mind of every man and thy
power is supreme : how then dost thou reconcile it
to thy mind to treat sinners and the just alike,
those whose mind's current sets to temperance and
those who incline to excess and trust in evil ways?"
" No certainty is vouchsafed by heaven to man, not
even to know what path of conduct is pleasing to
the gods ". " The thoughts of men are vain : they
know nothing. But the gods bring all things to pass
at their will : but yet the good man must endure and
bear all that comes ".

In the earlier dramatists we find the same phenomena still fully recognised. Especially prominent in
their thoughts is the mystery of inherited crime and
consequent suffering. The mystery of martyrdom is
also fully recognised. In one notable case we have
portrayed a divine or at least more than human

martyr. But in the treatment of the subject now, we find more attempt to justify the ways of GOD to men. The inherited curse and the suffering it brings are in a sense unmerited. But then whenever the suffering comes, it comes as punishment, punishment for sin born of the lawlessness which is the essence of the hereditary crime. Even in the person in whom the curse ends, whose suffering expiates the original guilt, whose sufferings might seem truly innocent, if not vicarious, even in him there is some irregularity, some human weakness, some want of absolute σωφροσύνη, some ignorance of the law of nemesis which provokes wrath and retribution. He shows as it were expiring flashes of the old ὕβρις; he takes the counsel of an inferior deity which jumps with his own human passion: he takes the retribution of heaven into his own hands, though it *is* the retribution of heaven; he chooses to act too willingly as a human Erinnys, and so brings the divine Erinnyes in full cry upon himself.

And in the case of dramas of martyrdom, whether of the demigod martyr, or the maiden-martyr, the suffering is not allowed to be quite innocent. The Titan is the noble and unselfish benefactor of human beings, the ignorant debased helpless and hopeless victims as it seems of the new sovereign of the gods. Unable to bear the sight of such oppressed misery he risks the wrath of Zeus and gives to mankind the necessaries of self-elevation, the raw material of civilization. But in the way he does it, he shows a spirit which gives a crook, as it were, to his benevolence. He shows a self-will which makes his heroism one-sided. Indifferent to the will of Zeus, careless to know his purposes, proud of possessing a secret about Zeus' destiny which Zeus himself does not share, he as hastily as stealthily assumes the rôle of tyrant opposer and champion of the oppressed, thwarting he knows not and cares not what far-reaching designs of Zeus and bringing on himself the necessary wrath of the thwarted king. And the maiden-martyr, the noblest creation of dramatic art, the sister who defied the law which did dishonour to her dead brother, the woman who appealed to the sovereign of the universe against the tyranny of man, to GOD against conventions, even she is not blameless of her own martyrdom. She is not free of offence against nemesis. She shows the γένιημ' ὠμὸν ἐξ ὠμοῦ πατρός: her womanhood has something fierce in it which sins against the Greek religion of μηδὲν ἄγαν. And in a sense she brings her doom upon herself, because however much she seems forced to do it, she takes her purpose by storm, takes the law of heaven into her own hands.

To put the matter summarily, the facts of suffering are fully recognised as a mystery, a mystery which there is some attempt to explain. At any rate there is attempt to justify the apparent injustice implied in

suffering. But the justification involves special plead-
ing. It proceeds in a vicious circle, because it assumes
the offender to be born an offender, yet punished with
suffering for committing the offence he was born to
commit, the only escape from this being a vague sense
of human free will which is rather felt than definitely
conceived or expressed.

Turning to Hebrew teachers we find the same
phenomena recognised, but naturally treated from a
somewhat different point of view. In the very earliest
time of the nation, we find the mystery of inherited
suffering recognised. But it is not regarded as the
effect of apathy or caprice on the part of the deity.
Nor is it the effect of an offence produced by the
originally begotten offence. It is the result of the
government of a GOD who is related to the nation,
between whom and the nation there exists a rela-
tionship of love. For the visiting of the sins of parents
on children to the third and fourth generations is
ascribed to the jealousy of GOD, the feeling of a
Being who will not let those whom He has brought
out of bondage revolt from Him, discard His allegiance,
commit fornication against Him, without punishing
until His offended justice has purged the tainted
blood. And so it was accepted as a truth that the
sins of parents must be expiated by their descendants,
and the truth was regarded as final and embodied
by after generations in a proverb. But the truth was

simply acquiesced in, misused as an excuse for deliberate sin, or recognised as the expression of the will of the jealous delivering GOD, according as his descendants could or could not keep fresh in their minds the teaching of the great legislator.

Later we have innocent suffering in its most general aspect treated as the subject of a religious drama, and the upshot of that treatment put briefly is (1) that suffering is compatible with innocence of life and (2) that it is a training and testing through which GOD puts His faithful servant, (3) lastly that it is beyond man's power to know the ways of that GOD, or to know the meaning of the discipline of unmerited suffering. He must be content to know that it is discipline and that it comes from the Father of all creation. But in the latter days of the kingdom and in the exile we begin to find the phenomenon of vicarious suffering recognised. In those latter days a sharp contrast developed between the faithless mass of the people (or perhaps more correctly the faithless worldly and corrupt upper part of the people) and the small remnant of Jehovah worshippers. This remnant suffers acutely from the sins of the faithless and suffers more acutely than they do, because it suffers all that they suffer, and besides that, suffers from the sight of their faithlessness, a pain to which they are insensible. This remnant moreover is destined to carry on the life of the nation, to be the vehicle of the

unfailing promises of GOD, is the true Israel. Out of
this contrast seems to emerge the conception of the
representative of the nation, the personification of the
true Israel, the Son of the nation, the man of sorrows
bruised for the transgressions of Israel, afflicted for the
sins of those who set him at naught and despised him,
yet carrying the life of the sinning nation through
the fire of the wrath of GOD, till it reappears purified
on the other side.

Thus in two representative peoples we find this
mystery of suffering exercising the minds of those
who cared to reflect on human destinies. We find
some common elements in these speculations: we find
the same acknowledgment that suffering may be
unmerited, that it comes on people from the faults
of others. We find the recognition of martyrdom in
both: we find suffering regarded by both as a means
of purification. But there is an essential difference.
The Greek apparently never recognised suffering as
possibly something in itself divine. Sufferers of all
kinds were subjects of the sovereign GOD Himself
exempt from suffering. In his highest conception of
the highest sufferer, when he has got beyond the crude
idea of a capricious deity who delights in human
suffering, he still finds the cause of suffering in the
human weakness, the human circumstance of each
sufferer. Suffering to him is entirely human. The
Hebrew through the suffering of his nation, in which

he seemed to see an innocent sufferer bearing the sins of offending kindred, found his way to the idea of divine suffering. This innocent sufferer for the sins of his nation grew in his mind into the divine Messiah, the man of sorrows anointed by GOD to bear the sins of many.

And so the Hebrew realised partially the truth of divine suffering. He realised that there is a suffering which is not simply a choice between two evils, the evil of suffering and the evil of giving up a high ideal, which is not simply good as punishment, not simply good as discipline, not even simply good as evidence of the paternal government of GOD—but which is good in itself as something which raises a man, something which the divine in man demands.

And we surely with the revelation of the Gospel of Jesus Christ in our hands—we cannot fall back on hedonism to help us in this matter. If we are to find life in this world we must surely find it in Him who revealed that GOD can suffer, that suffering is a part of the highest life that man can live. If to live is to know GOD, and we know Him in a suffering Son, we know that there is a suffering which is divine, that there is a suffering with Christ which is resurrection with Christ, we know that there is something in the highest nature of us that demands to die daily that it may live, something which reconciles us not only to suffering that comes to us from within ourselves but to suffering brought upon us by others, however it be brought. And not only reconciles us to it, but even brings us to rest and peace in bringing us into union with Christ, in bringing us to share His self-surrender, in bringing us to eat His flesh and drink His blood. We know that suffering to save others from suffering or to diminish the sum of human suffering, is the highest triumph of the Christ within us, an earnest of the Universal Triumph of Christ in all.

IV.

CHRIST THE JUDGING POWER IN MEN.

PHILIPPIANS I. 21.

To me to live is Christ.

ON the three Sundays past I have suggested three difficulties of human life, three problems that must more or less confront a human being trying to live what has always seemed to be the truly human life, which appeared to find solution in the belief that Christ the Son of GOD and the knowledge of GOD is the life of men. I should like to suggest one more fact on which this truth (if we may assume it such) seems to throw light, and to clear the path of practical men in their way through life. Now there is *consensu omnium* something in man by which he decides what is right and what is wrong, what he ought to do and what he ought not to do. Whether we are to call it moral sense, sense of obligation, sense of duty, or conscience is a question which must be left, I suppose,

where it has lain for some time, with those who
are competent to decide it. The other questions
connected with this thing; whether we are to call
it a faculty, or a function of the reason, whence it
derives, whether it is to be traced to the desire to
avoid pain and possess pleasure, whether this motive
acts directly, or indirectly, through the pains and
rewards dispensed by the majority of the society into
which a man is born, or whether it is something
which belongs to a man as such and is evoked and
evolved in contact with his fellowmen ; whether the
sense of right and wrong has become more or less
instinctive through the hereditary transmission of the
habit of identifying one's own interests with those of
the majority, or whether it is part of the nature of the
human being as organised to receive the inspiration of
the eternal consciousness ; these are questions which it
would be presumptuous on my part to attempt to deal
with before an Academic congregation. I will leave
therefore what I may call the philosophical questions
connected with this subject; I will say nothing to the
question whether the remotest ancestor of the conscience was fear of a whipping or of a toothache, I will
pass by the difficulty of understanding how likes can
produce unlikes, how the desire to avoid pains and
penalties can develop into the sense of the duty of
sacrificing one's own pleasures for the benefit of a
community, how the desire of reward can develop into

the feeling that one must bear any pains rather than assent to the wrongdoing of a majority, how fear of punishment can produce indignation at wrong, how in a word selfishness even crossed with tender emotions so called (themselves reducible ultimately to selfishness) can produce enthusiasm; I will leave, I say, these speculative and philosophical aspects of the subject to those who are competent to deal with them, and I will only speak shortly on two purely practical aspects of this fact of conscience (for so from predilection as well as for convenience sake I should prefer to call it) and see whether or how far it connects itself with the fact that St Paul enunciated when he said that to live to him was Christ.

Now this conscience, whatever it is and whencesoever it derives, is something which, as it now is, belongs absolutely to the individual. Without the first personal pronoun it could hardly be conceived of as existing. At the same time it cuts the 'I' in two. When a person says 'I ought to do this', or 'I ought not to have done that', he sits in judgment on himself; approves or condemns himself as the case may be. Moreover this judgment proceeds according to an authoritative standard of its own. Sometimes that standard coincides with the standard of the majority of the consciences with which the individual has been brought into contact; but sometimes it does not. Sometimes it agrees with only a small minority.

Sometimes it is in a minority of one. If this individual standard did not exist it would seem impossible
for moral progress to be made. For, however much
the general conscience (to use an intelligible and
convenient, but, I suppose, probably an unmeaning
term) may be tending towards a new standard of
opinion or feeling, however rapidly that new standard
may be adopted when once it is expressed and
formulated, it is individual consciences that really
introduce the new belief, thereby setting up a standard
different to the standard of the majority. Every step,
for example, in the progress from the establishment of
tribunals of justice to the abolition of duelling (the
progress which by the way is going on before long to
the abolition of duelling between nations which is
called war), every step in this progress must have been
a protest against the standard of action of a majority
in different places. Some one must have begun to say
' I ought not to fight, because I am a man and not at
present a tiger'. This being so, seeing that in some
most important cases the conscience is shown to be
wholly the individual's own, not a borrowed portion
of some general conscience, the standard it sets up
its own standard, not the standard of the majority,
it is a fair conclusion surely that this is so always:
that however much it may be educated by contact
with other consciences, however much it may gain
from such contact, what it gains is not borrowed but

appropriated, not loan or trust but gain of trading, that the individual conscience is the individual's own, that it judges him according to its own standard, has jurisdiction of its own, a court of its own, pronounces judgment upon him from which there is no appeal. And does it then pronounce judgment in its own cause? The answer to that question is I take it both 'yes' and 'no'. Inasmuch as the 'I' and the conscience are one, it does. But then (I speak only as a practical man, out of such experience as a practical man trying to live his life must get) these two are two as well as one. I need not apologise in this university for quoting one of its greatest sons, the prophetic man, who spent so fearlessly and ungrudgingly his vast resources of head and heart in winning souls to Christ. Prof. Maurice in his lectures on the conscience says "How can I know myself? Are there two creatures then, and I myself? It *does* sound monstrous. But monstrous or not these words [consciousness and conscience] involve that duplicity, they associate it with all my acts and thoughts, they remind me that I am stooping to the condition of a brute, not asserting my rights as a man, if I disavow it. For they are not words which belong to the inarticulate nomenclature of the savage: they are like the 'I', characteristic portions of organic civilised language; they appear in the discourses which have exercised most influence over bodies of men, as well as in those which discover the fears conflicts hopes, that belong to the secret chamber". And this division of the 'I', the duplicity of which Prof. Maurice speaks is a mystery, but a mystery of which those who must live their lives must find some sort of solution, at least some solution that will set them free to act. I find myself a being liable to passions desires propensions appetites, anxious to seek what is agreeable to me, to shun all that is painful to me. I find that the fact of living in a society checks these propensions to a certain extent, checks some and not others. Compels me in some cases to do what is painful, but allows me in others to indulge some of my worst propensities, especially, for example, my inclination to moral coward-ice. But I find another power, within me, which is myself and yet not myself, which is continually telling me 'I ought to do this, not to do that. I ought to indulge this feeling, check that feeling: I ought to incur this pain rather than do what is necessary to avoid it'. I find this power continually thus judging me, putting me on my trial in spite of myself, convict-ing me of wrong when I want to think myself right, making right clear when I want to think it wrong. I find it judging me and punishing me, passing sentence of shame and remorse upon me, when it has brought in a verdict of guilty against me.

This is one very practical aspect of this thing

conscience, that it divides a man when it is present against himself, that it speaks to him with an authority he cannot dispute, when it does speak and he listens, judging him, approving or condemning him and always satisfying him, at least when he is listening to it at his best, that its verdict is a true one.

There is another aspect equally practical. This conscience, this judging power may lie apparently dormant in a man. It may be like an unused faculty: it may be apparently absent from him. A man may go on living for years, for the greater part of his life even, without ever being taken to task by himself, conscienceless in fact. And yet quite unlike an unused faculty or instinct, which perishes by want of use, this judging power will revive, reappear in full force at a moment's notice, suddenly, generally unexpectedly: and when it reappears it will light up the whole life from one end to the other, rouse long forgotten events and feelings out of their obscurity and bring them into the full light of present facts and feelings. Professor Maurice instances as illustrating the power of conscience to bind the different parts of man's existence together the story of Œdipus and Laius. He points out how the consciousness of what he had really done when he killed Laius only awoke in Œdipus years after he had committed the murder, how the consciousness of the act he had done so long before rose up years after to convict him of parricide. In this case of course there was not an apparent absence of the power of conscience generally in the life during a long interval followed by subsequent reappearance which is rather the point which I have ventured to suggest as important. Perhaps as good an illustration as any of this may be found in Shakespere's Richard III. A character drawn by him I may assume, I suppose, to be, however historically incorrect, humanly consistent and true. Here we have apparently a perfectly conscience-less man, one who has carried out a purely selfish purpose in life regardless of any 'I ought' or 'I ought not'. But just at the end of his life when he seems to want the fullest and most concentrated selfishness and consciencelessness, to save himself from failure, this conscience revives in him, raises trial within him, judges, condemns him, and strikes him powerless. It seems to light up all the disregarded facts of his life which now are raised up against him as present facts, parts of his existence linked together by the conscience newly sprung upon him to judge him.

> 'O coward conscience, how dost thou afflict me!
> My conscience hath a thousand several tongues
> And every tongue brings in a several tale,
> And every tale condemns me for a villain'.
>
> . . . .
>
> 'I shall despair. There is no creature loves me.
> And if I die, no soul shall pity me.
> Nay wherefore should they, since that I myself
> Find in myself no pity for myself'.

Perhaps I may be allowed to quote another illus-

tration from another master of human nature, one of
our own time, a man of true prophetic insight and true
Christian belief in human nature, Charles Dickens.
Among his earlier sketches is one called 'The hospital
patient', a sketch from nature apparently. A girl has
been terribly injured by a lowlived ruffianly paramour.
In consequence of a question raised as to the identity
of the prisoner, it is arranged that he shall accompany
the magistrates when they go to take the woman's
deposition. At the time arranged he is taken to the
hospital and to the bedside of the patient. The girl as
soon as she saw him with one convulsive effort started
up: then falling back on her pillow and covering her
scarred and bruised face with her hands burst into
tears. 'The man', says the author, 'cast an anxious
look towards her, but otherwise appeared wholly un-
moved'. Then the oath was administered, and she was
asked to make her statement. But instead of doing
this, she broke out into wild protestations of the man's
innocence. 'I did it myself: it was an accident: he
didn't hurt me: he wouldn't do it for all the world'.
Then turning to the man and addressing him by name,
'You know you wouldn't'. But he knew he had, and
knew now on a sudden *what* it was that he had done.
'For', continues Dickens, 'brute as he was, the man
was not prepared for this: he turned his face from the
bed and sobbed'. It was not fear now that moved
him, which I suppose was the meaning of that anxious

look mentioned before. Fear does not make a man cry. There was something came upon this man and raised a feeling which overpowered every other feeling, subdued every selfish fear and filled him with an overwhelming despair. It was conscience that suddenly revisited him, lighted up his life and fetched out of dark places old feelings long forgotten, which confronted him each with a several tongue condemning him.

Now these are two facts of everyday practical life, (1) that there is a power in us which is capable of dividing us against ourselves, which has an authority of its own whereby it puts us on our trial within our own minds, judges us, and passes sentence upon us; (2) that this power though it seems able, as it were, to disappear, to lie in abeyance for a length of time which would materially impair the force of any ordinary faculty of the mind or soul, will reappear in full vigour, exercise all its functions with unimpaired force, and when it reappears not only sets up a sudden unexpected tribunal, but lighting up the whole life will bring into court a thousand dark forgotten facts to speak as living present witnesses against us.

Now with two such facts as these continually facing him, what is a practical man to do? If he were watching life out of study window, he might be content to speculate about possible human origins of this power of conscience. But if he is living his life in the midst

of men and women, obliged to be perpetually facing
cases of conscience, as they are called, obliged to take
the verdict of this inward judge; if he is obliged
sometimes to take a verdict about his own conduct
which sets him in opposition to the opinion of the
majority of those about him, forces him, it may be,
to oppose the embodied traditions and beliefs of
society; can such a one be satisfied to live with such
a power, as this conscience is, at work about him,
unless he can believe that it is something, which, if it
is himself, is something more than himself, something
outside himself as well as within himself, something
human and not human, a union within him of the
human and the divine? Will he not demand that such
an authority, if he must obey it, as it seems he must,
should be the authority not of a development, a
function, a faculty, or of any abstraction, but of a
person, a master, in whose control he can find freedom,
a master who will never let him quite loose from his
control, who if a man forgets Him, ignores Him, and
makes of His master's dwelling-place a house of his
own, will visit him in an hour that he knoweth not?
Will he not fall back on St Paul's words in regard
to this matter as to others, and find that he cannot
live his life unless he finds his life in Christ? If with
St Paul he believes that life is knowledge of GOD,
consciousness of union with GOD, he will surely like
St Paul look to find that knowledge in Christ. For

desiring the word of GOD and reading the record of the
life and death of Jesus Christ he will surely jump the
difficulties of historic or philosophic doubt. He will say
'here is what I want to enable me not to philosophise
but to live: here is the word of GOD given to men in
a man: here is the GOD-man, the Son of GOD, master
of men. And if he persuades himself of this, then,
I suppose, the conscience, the power that divides
him, sifts him, tries him, will seem to him a power of
Christ, of Christ the Judge to whom the Father has
committed all judgment; Christ the patient Judge who
stands at the door and knocks and if any one will open
to Him will enter in and dwell with that man, holding
His court in his heart; Christ the Judge, who, if a man
will not hear and open to Him, will suddenly visit His
temple and will show to that man a day of the Son of
man, when the light that lightens every man that
cometh into the world, suddenly illumines the whole
heaven to him, flashes from one end of his life to the
other and judges him down. Thus I fancy will the
man, who can persuade himself that Christ is life to
him, satisfy himself about this conscience, this judging
power. He will regard it (whatever its philosophic
origin) as a living present fact, of which the living
present explanation is the life of Christ.

In discharging the duty entrusted to me of
Christian preacher for this year I have tried to show

that the revelation of Christ answers some of the
most anxious life-questions which force themselves on
human beings living in the midst of the active life
of the world. The description of the duty of the
Christian Preacher, viz. ' to show evidence for Revealed
Religion', seemed to leave practically open to me
only one of two alternatives, either to deal with
external and objective evidence of the historical truth
of the records of our religion, or with the subjective
evidence of it, the evidence for it existing in human
nature. To attempt the former in a University bristling
with Biblical teaching and criticism, would have been
out of place in an outsider. In confining myself to
the connexion between the wants of human nature
and the offers of the Gospel, I have been able to
speak out of that experience which must be each
man's own. And I have gained an opportunity of
adding my humble testimony to a fact which I think
needs to be borne in mind as much now as ever,
viz. that (to put it concisely) no amount of external
testimony to the genuineness of the Christian records
can ever produce Christian faith : that valuable as
such evidence is to a believer he must be a believer
before it is valuable to him; that Christian faith must
spring from the testimony of the human heart to
which the Gospel irresistibly approves itself. I cannot
express my meaning half so well in my own words as
in the words of one to whom I have referred before in

my first Sermon, 'An assent to propositions on evidence is no intrinsic element in Christian Faith : its object is not past events but a present reconciled and indwelling GOD. Its interest in the work of Christ is in this as a finished work, i.e. in present relations with GOD which Christ's work is thought to have rendered possible. It is no doubt historically conditioned; but it is not on an intellectual estimate of its own conditions that it depends for being what it is. Without the Christian tradition it would not be what it is, but a judgment as to the authenticity of that tradition is not essential to it as a spiritual state. Controversy compels the faithful to justify their faith. In its true nature Faith can be justified by nothing by itself'.